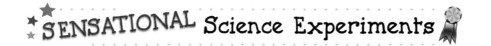
SENSATIONAL Science Experiments

Split-Second Science Projects with Speed

How Fast Does It Go?

Robert Gardner

Enslow Publishers, Inc.

40 Industrial Road	PO Box 38
Box 398	Aldershot
Berkeley Heights, NJ 07922	Hants GU12 6BP
USA	UK

http://www.enslow.com

Library of Congress Cataloging-in-Publication Data

Gardner, Robert, 1929–
    Split-second science projects with speed : How fast does it go? / Robert Gardner.
       p. cm. — (Sensational science experiments)
    Includes bibliographical references and index.
    ISBN 0-7660-2017-7
    1. Speed—Experiments—Juvenile literature. [1. Speed—Experiments.
2. Experiments. 3. Science projects.] I. Title. II. Series.
    QC137.5 .G37 2003
    531'.112'078—dc21

                                         2002004618

Printed in the United States of America

10 9 8 7 6 5 4 3 2 1

Illustration credits: Tom LaBaff

Cover illustrations: Tom LaBaff

Contents

(Experiments with a 🎗 symbol feature **Ideas for Your Science Fair.**)

Introduction

What do you think of when you hear the word "speed"? A race car zooming around a track at 200 miles per hour? A cheetah in Africa chasing its dinner? A shooting star streaking through Earth's atmosphere?

Chances are, when you hear the word "speed," you think of things that go fast. You probably do not think of a snail inching along a branch or an autumn leaf floating to the ground.

But speed does not describe only things that go fast—it is a measure of how fast things go. The speed of even the slowest moving things can be measured.

Simply put, speed is the measure of how far something goes and how long it takes to get there. How far—the distance—can be measured in anything from millimeters to miles. How long—the time—can be measured in anything from seconds to decades. Speed is **distance** and **time** combined.

Let's get a feel for measuring speed. If you rode your bike for an hour and you traveled ten miles, what was your average speed? (We say "average" because you probably went slower up hills and faster down them.) Your average speed was ten miles per hour. Simple, right?

Here is a harder one. If you walked six miles in two hours, what was your average speed in miles per hour? The answer is three miles per hour.

6 miles ÷ 2 hours = 3 miles per hour

If you got that, good going. If not, do not worry about it. By the time you are done reading this book and having fun with the experiments in it, you will be a speed demon.

In some of the experiments, you will measure average speed. To do that, you will measure the distance something moved and the time it took to move that distance. Then you will divide the distance by the time. The answer is the average speed, which is what we found above.

Try one more. This time use the metric system to measure the distance. Suppose you ran for one hour and then walked for one hour and you went twenty kilometers. What was your average speed? The answer is ten kilometers per hour. Remember the formula for average speed? Distance divided by time. So to figure out the above question, you would write:

distance ÷ time = speed
20 kilometers ÷ 2 hours = 10 kilometers per hour

As you know, speeds can range from very slow to very fast. Snails reach a top speed of about 164 feet per hour. Light is the fastest moving thing ever measured. It travels at 300,000 kilometers in one second! Sounds move through air at about 330 meters per second, which is only one-millionth as fast as light. That is why when you are sitting in the top row of a stadium, you can see the batter hit the ball before you can hear the ball hitting the bat.

Entering a Science Fair

Some of the experiments in this book might give you ideas for a science fair project. Those experiments are marked with a symbol 🎗. Remember, judges at science fairs like experiments that are imaginative. It is hard to be creative unless you are interested in your project. So pick a subject that you enjoy and want to know more about.

If you use an experiment in this book for a science fair project, be sure to change it or extend it. As you do the experiments in this book, you will think of your own experiments that could make excellent science fair projects. And because the ideas are yours, you will find them more interesting than any you read about.

If you enter a science fair, you should read some of

the books listed in the back of this book. They will give you helpful hints and lots of useful information about science fairs. You will learn how to prepare great reports. You will also learn how to set up and display your work, how to present your project, and how to talk with judges and visitors.

Safety First

As you do the activities and experiments in this or any other book, do them safely. Remember the rules listed below and follow them closely.

1. Any experiments that you do should be done under the supervision of a parent, teacher, or another adult.

2. Read all instructions carefully. If you have questions, check with an adult. Do not take chances.

3. If you work with a friend who enjoys science too, keep a serious attitude while experimenting. Fooling around can be dangerous to you and to others.

4. Keep the area where you are experimenting clean and organized. When you have finished, clean up and put away the materials you were using.

Speedometer

The word "meter" comes from the Greek word *metron*, which means "measure." A speedometer is a tool that measures speed. There is one on a car's dashboard.

Let's Get Started!

1. When you are a passenger in a car, watch the speedometer. Speedometers usually have a pointer that moves along a dial. Most speedometers measure speed in kilometers per hour (kph) and miles per hour (mph). If the speedometer reads 100 kilometers per hour, what is the reading in miles per hour? If the speedometer reads 50 miles per hour, what is the reading in kilometers per hour?

2. What is the reading on the speedometer when the car is at rest? What happens to the speedometer reading when the adult driver steps on the gas pedal? Is the speedometer reading ever steady (unchanging)? If so, under what conditions is it steady?

3. Watch the car's speedometer the next time you make a short trip. What was the fastest speed at which the car moved? Did the speed stay the same during the trip? When did the car's speed increase? When did it decrease?

Readings

What happens to the car's speed as it approaches a stoplight or a stop sign? What happens to the car's speed after a stoplight turns green or the car has stopped at an intersection?

An Odometer

Near the speedometer on a car's dashboard is another tool, called an odometer. An odometer measures how far a car has gone along the road.

Let's Get Started!

1. The next time you are a car passenger, write down the numbers (miles) on the odometer and the time you begin your journey. The odometer will record the number of miles that the car travels. At the end of your trip, again write down the number of miles on the odometer and the time.

Things you will need:
- ✔ car with an odometer
- ✔ watch
- ✔ notebook and pencil
- ✔ an ADULT
- ✔ calculator

2. Subtract the beginning odometer reading from the final odometer reading. This will give you the number of miles you traveled. How far did you go?

3. Use the odometer to measure the distance you travel on each trip you take in a car this year. What was your longest trip? Your shortest trip?

4. You can also measure the car's average speed using the odometer and a watch. At the beginning of a trip,

and a Clock

record the odometer reading and the time. After half an hour, record the odometer reading. How far did you go? How far would you go in an hour at the same speed? What was your average speed during the half-hour trip?

Walking

How fast do you walk? To find out, you can measure the distance you walk in 15 minutes.

Let's Get Started!

1 You will count the number of times you walk around the perimeter (outside lines) of a football field in 15 minutes. A football field's perimeter is about 310 meters (340 yards, or 1,020 feet). To do this, record the time when you begin your walk. After fifteen minutes, stop walking and record the number of times you walked around the field.

2 Suppose you walked around the field three and a half times. The total distance you walked is:

$$\textbf{310 meters x } 3\tfrac{1}{2} \textbf{ = 1,085 meters}$$

Fifteen minutes is one fourth of an hour, so you could expect to walk four times as far in an hour. Since 4 x 1,085 meters = 4,340 meters, you would expect to go 4,340 meters in one hour. Your walking speed would be 4,340 meters per hour. What is your walking speed in meters per second? (**Hint**: Divide the answer by 3600, since there are 3600 seconds in an hour.)

Speeds

How fast do your friends walk? How fast do your parents walk?

How does your walking speed compare with your running speed? You can find out by doing the next experiment.

Running

How fast can you run? To find out, you can measure the time it takes you to run 50 meters. Fifty meters is approximately 55 yards, so you can use 55 yards on a football field as a distance of 50 meters. A friend can time you with a stopwatch or a watch with a second hand.

Let's Get Started!

1. Before you run, do some stretching and jogging to warm up your leg muscles. When you have warmed up, take a sprinter's stance on the goal line.

2. Have your friend stand 5 yards beyond the 50-yard line. Your friend will raise his arm. When his arm comes quickly down, you will start to run and he will start timing. He will note the time when you cross the line he is standing on.

A well-trained sprinter can run 50 meters in about 6 seconds. His speed would be:

50 meters ÷ 6 seconds = $8\frac{1}{3}$ meters per second

How many seconds did it take you to run 50 meters? What is your running speed in meters per second?

Speeds

Ideas for Your Science Fair

How does your running speed compare with that of a well-trained sprinter?

How fast can your friends run? Who can run the fastest?

What is your speed for a 100-meter sprint?

Things you will need:
- ✔ football field
- ✔ stopwatch or watch with second hand
- ✔ notebook and pencil
- ✔ friends

Animals: Fast

S ome animals move very fast. Other animals move slowly. How does your running speed compare with the speeds of the animals listed below?

Animal	SPEED			Animal	SPEED		
	kilometers per hour	meters per second	miles per hour		kilometers per hour	meters per second	miles per hour
Cheetah	97	26.9	60	Elephant	41	11.4	25
Lion	81	22.5	50	Snake (Black mamba)	32	8.9	20
Coyote	70	19.4	43	Pig	18	5.0	11
Greyhound	65	18.1	40	Chicken	15	4.2	9
Horse	61	16.9	38	Spider	1.9	0.53	1.2
Rabbit	57	15.8	35	Tortoise (Giant)	.27	0.08	.17
Bear (Grizzly)	49	13.6	30	Snail	.05	0.01	.03

Which of the animals can run faster than a well-trained sprinter such as the one mentioned in the last experiment?

How fast can your (or a friend's) dog run?

and Slow

Things you will need:
- ✔ friend
- ✔ your dog or a friend's dog
- ✔ football field
- ✔ stopwatch or watch with a second hand

Let's Get Started!

① Have a friend hold the dog on the goal line of a football field while you stand on the opposite goal line.

② Call the dog as your friend releases it. As the dog starts to run, start a stopwatch. When the dog reaches you, stop the stopwatch.

Suppose it takes the dog 15 seconds to run the 100 yards (300 feet) between you and your friend. The animal's speed was:

300 feet ÷ 15 seconds = 20 feet per second

To find the dog's speed in miles per hour, multiply by 0.68.

20 feet per second x 0.68 = 13.6 miles per hour

How fast can other dogs run?

Wind Speeds

In 1806, Sir Francis Beaufort developed a way to estimate the speed of the wind. He observed things happening around him while the wind blew at certain speeds. His method, known as the Beaufort scale, is shown in the illustrations on pages 19–21.

Things you will need:
- ✔ Beaufort scale
- ✔ calendar
- ✔ clock
- ✔ notebook and pencil

Let's Get Started!

1. Using the Beaufort scale, estimate the wind speed at different times of the day for a month or two. It would be even better to estimate the wind speeds for a year. Record your results in a notebook.

Many people say that March is the windiest month. Do you find this is true? If not, which month do you find to be the windiest?

Do you find a common time during most days when wind speeds are fastest? Do you find a common time during most days when wind speeds are slowest?

Do wind speeds tend to increase during a rainstorm or a snowstorm?

What is the fastest wind you have observed?

by Observation

Ideas for Your Science Fair

Go to a library and do some research. Where in the world are wind speeds greatest? Where in the United States are wind speeds greatest? What is the highest wind speed ever recorded?

The Beaufort Scale

Beaufort scale number: **0**

Observations: **calm; smoke goes straight up; can't feel wind on face**

Estimated wind speed:

kph	mph
0–1.5	0–1

Beaufort scale number: **1**

Observations: **light wind; smoke drifts slowly with wind**

Estimated wind speed:

kph	mph
1.6–5	1.1–3

Beaufort scale number: **2**

Observations: **wind can be felt on face; leaves rustle; flags and weather vanes move**

Estimated wind speed:

kph	mph
6–11	4–7

Beaufort scale number: **3**

Observations: **gentle breeze; leaves and small twigs move; flags begin to extend outward**

Estimated wind speed: **kph** **mph**
12–19 **8–12**

Beaufort scale number: **4**

Observations: **moderate breeze; dust and small papers blow about; small branches move; flags flap**

Estimated wind speed: **kph** **mph**
20–29 **13–18**

Beaufort scale number: **5**

Observations: **fresh breeze; small trees sway; flags ripple; whitecaps on inland waters**

Estimated wind speed: **kph** **mph**
30–38 **19–24**

Beaufort scale number: **6**

Observations: **strong breeze; large branches move; flags beat; telephone wires whistle**

Estimated wind speed: **kph** **mph**
39–50 **25–31**

Beaufort scale number: **7**

Observations: **strong wind; whole trees move; flags extended; walking in wind a bit difficult**

Estimated wind speed: **kph** **mph**
51–61 **32–38**

Beaufort scale number: **8**

Observations: **gale winds; twigs break off trees; walking in wind is difficult**

Estimated wind speed:

kph	mph
62–74	39–46

Beaufort scale number: **9**

Observations: **strong gale; slight damage to buildings; tiles or shingles may be torn off roofs**

Estimated wind speed:

kph	mph
75–86	47–54

Beaufort scale number: **10**

Observations: **storm winds; small trees uprooted; roofs damaged**

Estimated wind speed:

kph	mph
87–100	55–63

Beaufort scale number: **11**

Observations: **violent storm winds; widespread damage**

Estimated wind speed:

kph	mph
101–118	64–74

Beaufort scale number: **12**

Observations: **hurricane winds; extensive damage**

Estimated wind speed:

kph	mph
>118	>74

Wind Speeds

You can make a meter to measure wind speeds.

Let's Get Started!

1 Find a smooth square piece of wood about 15 centimeters (6 inches) on a side. Hammer nails partway into two corners of the wood as shown.

Things you will need:
- ✔ square piece of plywood about 15 centimeters (6 inches) on a side
- ✔ hammer
- ✔ nails
- ✔ tin snips
- ✔ tin can
- ✔ ruler
- ✔ pliers
- ✔ an ADULT
- ✔ calm day
- ✔ straight road with very little traffic
- ✔ windy days

2 **Ask an adult** to use tin snips to cut a strip of metal from a tin can. The strip should be about one inch wide and 8 inches long. Pliers can be used to bend one end of the strip around the upper nail. When the meter is pointed into the wind, the metal strip will be pushed up at an angle.

3 To measure wind speeds, you must calibrate (mark the speeds on) the meter. To do this, **ask an adult** to take you for a car ride on a calm day. On a straight road where there is little traffic, ask the driver to go exactly 10 miles per hour. The car moving through still air creates a wind. Hold the meter out of the window. The metal strip will be pushed to the side. Use a pencil to mark on the wood how far the strip is pushed from its rest position. Repeat this process when the car is traveling at 20, 30, 40, and 50 miles per hour.

4 On a windy day, test your meter. How closely does your meter agree with the Beaufort scale?

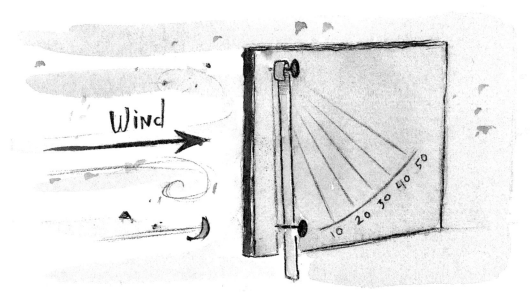

Idea for Your Science Fair

Which method do you think is the more accurate measure of wind speed?

Wind Direction

Speed and velocity are not the same. Speed is how far something goes in a certain time. Velocity is speed in a certain direction. A car going north at 80 kilometers per hour has a speed of 80 kilometers per hour. It has a velocity of 80 kilometers per hour north.

To find wind velocity you need to know its direction. You can find wind direction by building a weather vane. It will point toward the direction of the wind.

Things you will need:

✔ an ADULT
✔ piece of plywood, 6 inches x 16 inches x ½ inch thick
✔ long, thin screw and washer
✔ drill and bit
✔ coping saw or jigsaw
✔ 2-inch x 4-inch post, 5½ feet tall
✔ shovel
✔ wind meter from last experiment

Let's Get Started!

1. **Ask an adult** to cut an arrow from a piece of plywood.

2. Move the arrow back and forth on your finger until it balances. **Ask an adult** to drill a hole through the arrow at this spot. Use a drill bit slightly larger than the screw you will use to attach the weather vane to a post. A washer between the post and the weather vane allows the vane to spin easily.

and Velocity

3. Bury the bottom end of the post in a hole about 18 inches deep.

4. Mount the vane on the wooden post. The post should be out in the open. If you do not know directions (north, south, east, and west) around your house or school, ask a parent or teacher to show you.

5. Use your weather vane and wind meter to find wind velocities. What is the usual wind direction where you live?

Autumn's beauty fades as colorful leaves fall from their trees. Unlike stones or baseballs, leaves fall slowly. How slowly do they fall?

Let's Get Started!

1 Ask a friend to drop a leaf from a known height when you say, "Drop!" As you speak, start a stopwatch or look at the second hand on your watch. When the leaf reaches the ground, stop the stopwatch or note the position of the second hand on your watch.

Things you will need:
✔ a friend
✔ stopwatch or watch with second hand
✔ calculator
✔ leaves of different size
✔ 2 pieces of paper

2 Use a calculator to find the speed at which the leaf fell. Remember: **speed = distance ÷ time**.

Do all leaves fall at the same speed? Do big leaves fall faster than small leaves?

3 Why do leaves fall so slowly? Could it be the amount of surface exposed to air? You can do an experiment to find out. Take two pieces of paper. Squeeze one piece into a tight wad. Leave the other piece open. Drop both pieces of paper from the same height at

Falling Leaves

the same time. Which one falls faster? Which one has to push more air aside?

Idea for Your Science Fair

Place one piece of paper on a book that is larger than the paper. Hold another piece by itself. Release the book with the paper on it and the other piece of paper from the same height at the same time. Which falls faster?

Speed and

After falling for a few seconds, a sky diver reaches a speed of nearly 200 kilometers per hour (120 miles per hour) through the air. To reduce his speed, the sky diver pulls a cord that opens his parachute. The parachute acts like a large sheet of paper in air. It reduces the sky diver's speed so he can land safely on the ground.

You can make a simple parachute to see how it reduces the speed at which something falls. You will need four pieces of thread, each about 30 centimeters (12 inches) long.

Things you will need:
- ✔ 8 pieces of thread, each about 30 centimeters (12 inches) long
- ✔ 2 large handkerchiefs
- ✔ 2 metal washers
- ✔ rubber band

Let's Get Started!

1 Tie the ends of each piece of thread to the corners of a large handkerchief. Tie the other ends of the threads to a metal washer. The washer represents the sky diver.

2 Make a second identical parachute. Use a rubber band to hold all the parts of this second parachute closely together, so it will not open. Fold the first parachute and

Parachutes

wrap the threads loosely around it with the washer on the outside. Close your hands around both parachutes.

3) Throw both up into the air so they reach approximately the same height. Compare the speeds at which the two parachutes return to the ground.

Growth

How fast are you growing? To find out, ask a friend or parent to measure your height on the first day of every month for at least a year.

1 Tape a sheet of paper to a door frame. The center of the paper should be as high as the top of your head.

2 Take off your shoes and stand up very straight with your back against the door frame.

3 Have your friend hold a ruler or yardstick across the top of your head. The ruler should be level, with one end pushing against the paper. The person holding the ruler can use

Speed

a pencil to mark where the ruler touches the paper.

④ The distance from the floor to the mark is your height. Measure this distance with a meterstick, yardstick, or tape measure. How tall are you in centimeters? In meters and centimeters? In inches? In feet and inches? Record your height and the date in a notebook each time you make a measurement.

Things you will need:
✔ friend or parent
✔ tape
✔ paper
✔ door frame
✔ ruler or yardstick
✔ notebook and pencil
✔ meterstick, yardstick, or tape measure

⑤ How tall are you a month later? A year later? To find your growth speed, divide your change in height by the time between measurements. If, in one month, you grew from 120 cm to 123 cm, you grew at a speed of:

3 centimeters ÷ 1 month = 3 centimeters per month

or

3 centimeters ÷ 30 days = 0.1 centimeters per day, or 1 millimeter per day

What is your growth speed over a year's time?

You know your fingernails grow because you have to cut them. But how fast do they grow?

Let's Get Started!

1. Use the edge of a fingernail file to scratch a short straight line across a thumbnail, just in front of the cuticle. The cuticle is skin that surrounds the base of your fingernail. Measure the distance from the scratch to the bottom edge of the white band at the end of the nail. Record the measurement and the date in a notebook.

2. A week later, measure the distance from the scratch to the white band again. Has the scratch moved closer to the band? Subtract your second measurement from your first to find out how much your nail grew in one week. Continue to do this on the same day each week. (You may have to refile the scratch occasionally to keep it visible.)

    How fast does your nail grow in millimeters per week? In millimeters per month?

Ideas for Your Science Fair
Which grows faster, your fingernails or you?

Fingernails Grow?

Do all your fingernails grow at the same speed? Do they grow faster than your toenails? Do they grow faster in summer than in winter?

Do everyone's fingernails grow at the same speed?

Do girls' fingernails grow faster than boys'?

Design an experiment to find out how fast your hair grows.

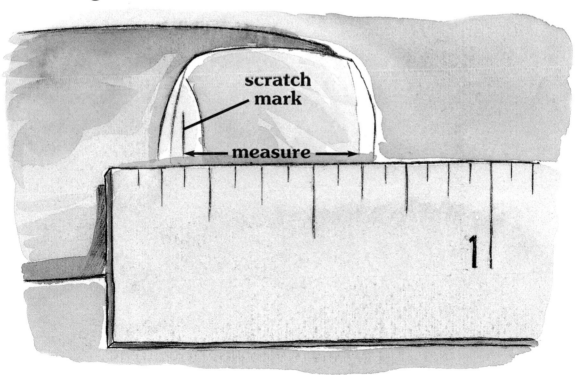

scratch mark

← measure →

1

How Fast Do

How fast do you read? Reading speed, or reading rate, as you might guess, is measured in words per minute.

1 Ask a friend to time you as you read the introduction of this book. Start reading silently when your friend says, "Go!" Continue to read until one minute has passed and your friend says, "Stop!" Put your finger on the last word you read. Then count the number of words you read. What is your reading speed in words per minute?

2 Repeat the experiment, but this time read aloud. Do you read faster silently or aloud?

Things you will need:
✔ a friend
✔ stopwatch or watch with second hand
✔ notebook and pencil
✔ book

3 Find a book that you think you might like to read. Read that book for 10 minutes and, again, figure out your reading speed. You do not have to count all the words. Count the words on one page and multiply that by the number of pages you read in 10 minutes.

You Read?

Ideas for Your Science Fair

Is your reading speed over a 10-minute period the same as or different from your speed over a 1-minute period?

Borrow an eighth-grade reading book and a second-grade reading book. Measure your reading speed using first one book and then the other. How does the reading level of the book affect your reading speed? How does it affect your ability to understand what you read?

Speed of

What affects the speed at which ice melts? You can measure the melting speed of ice quite easily.

Let's Get Started!

1 Place an ice cube in half a glass of water. If the ice cube is completely melted in 10 minutes, you can say the melting speed was:

1 cube ÷ 10 minutes = 1 cube per 10 minutes, or 0.1 cube per minute

2 Do you think the amount of water around the ice cube will affect its melting speed? To find out, fill a plastic bucket with water.

3 Remove half a glass of water from the bucket. In this way you can be sure the temperature of the water in both glass and bucket are the same.

4 Place an ice cube in the half glass of water. At the same time place an identical ice cube in the bucket of water. In which container is the melting speed faster?

Why was it important to use identical ice cubes (cubes with the same size and shape)? Why was it important to be sure the water temperatures in the two containers were the same?

Melting

Ideas for Your Science Fair

Do you think the temperature of the water will affect the melting speed of ice? Design an experiment to find out.

Do you think the shape of the ice will affect its melting speed? Design an experiment to find out.

Things you will need:
- ✔ ice cubes of the same size and shape
- ✔ water glasses
- ✔ stopwatch or watch with second hand
- ✔ hot and cold tap water
- ✔ plastic bucket

Speed of

If you add a little sugar to a glass of water, the sugar slowly disappears. We say the sugar "dissolves" in the water. Or we might say, the sugar is "soluble" in water. Does water temperature affect the speed at which sugar dissolves in water? Does the amount of water affect the speed at which sugar dissolves in water?

Let's Get Started!

1. Fill a drinking glass about three fourths of the way with cold tap water.

2. Pour the same amount of hot tap water into an identical glass.

3. Add a sugar cube to each glass at the same time. Use soda straws to gently stir the water in both glasses. In which glass does the sugar dissolve fastest? How does water temperature affect the speed at which sugar dissolves?

4. Fill a quart container with warm tap water.

5. Pour some of the warm water into a drinking glass until it is nearly filled.

> **Things you will need:**
> - 2 identical drinking glasses
> - hot and cold tap water
> - several sugar cubes
> - soda straws
> - 1-quart container

Dissolving

6. Fill an identical glass about one third of the way with the warm water.

7. Add a sugar cube to each glass at the same time. Gently stir the water in both glasses. In which glass does the sugar dissolve fastest? How does the amount of water affect the speed at which sugar dissolves?

Idea for Your Science Fair

Design an experiment to find out how the dissolving speeds for equal weights of sugar and salt compare.

Speed While

When something falls, does its speed remain the same throughout the fall? Or does its speed get faster as it falls?

To find out, you will drop an object, such as a baseball, from different heights and measure the time it takes to fall to the ground. If an object's speed stays the same during a fall, it should take twice as long to fall twice as far, three times as long to fall three times as far, and so on. You can use a stopwatch to measure time.

Let's Get Started!

1. Hold the object 1 meter or 1 yard above the floor. Start the stopwatch the instant you release the ball. Stop the watch the moment the ball strikes the ground. Repeat your measurements several times until they are consistent. (It takes a little time to get the hang of starting and stopping the watch.)

2. Drop the ball from a height of 2 meters or 2 yards. Does it take twice as long to fall 2 meters or 2 yards?

3. **Ask an adult** to help you measure the time it takes for a ball to fall 4 meters or 4 yards. A second-story

Falling

window will probably provide the height needed. Does the object take four times as long to fall four times as far?

What do your results tell you about the speed of falling objects? Does the speed stay the same or does it change?

Speed of a

When placed in water, a seltzer tablet reacts chemically. It forms bubbles of carbon dioxide. We say the tablet "fizzes" in water.

Let's Get Started!

1 Drop a seltzer tablet into half a glass of water. Measure the time it takes for the entire tablet to stop fizzing. The speed of the reaction is how long it takes the tablet to dissolve. What is the speed of the reaction in tablets per minute?

Things you will need:
- ✔ cold and hot tap water
- ✔ seltzer tablets
- ✔ water glasses
- ✔ stopwatch or watch with second hand

2 Drop two tablets into another half glass of water. Is the speed of the reaction the same? That is, does the reaction take twice as long? If not, what is the speed of the reaction?

3 Does the amount of water affect the speed of the reaction? To find out, drop a seltzer tablet into half a glass of water. At the same time, drop another tablet into a full glass of water. Do both reactions go at the same speed? If not, how does the amount of water affect the speed of the reaction?

4 Does the temperature of the water affect the speed of

Chemical Reaction

the reaction? Fill one glass halfway with cold tap water. Fill a second identical glass halfway with hot tap water. Drop a tablet into each glass at the same time. Do both reactions go at the same speed? If not, how does temperature affect the speed of the reaction?

Idea for Your Science Fair
What would you do to make the reaction go as fast as possible?

Words to Know

average speed—Total distance traveled divided by total time of travel.

Beaufort scale—A way of estimating wind speed by observing flags, trees, and other outdoor objects.

odometer—A device that measures distance traveled.

parachute—A device used to increase air resistance after a person jumps from a high altitude, such as from an airplane.

speed—Distance traveled in a certain time.

speedometer—A device that measures speed.

velocity—Speed and direction of motion.

Further Reading

Bochinski, Julianne Blair. *The Complete Handbook of Science Fair Projects*. New York: John Wiley & Sons, 1996.

Bombaugh, Ruth. *Science Fair Success, Revised and Expanded*. Springfield, N.J.: Enslow Publishers, Inc., 1999.

Markle, Sandra. *The Young Scientist's Guide to Successful Science Projects*. New York: Lothrop, Lee, and Shepard, 1990.

Markle, Sandra. *Measuring Up: Experiments, Puzzles, and Games Exploring Measurement*. New York: Atheneum, 1995.

Smoothey, Marion. *Estimating*. New York: Marshall Cavendish, 1994.

Tocci, Salvatore. *How to Do a Science Fair Project*. Revised Edition. Danbury, Conn.: Franklin Watts, 1997.

Walpole, Brenda. *Measuring Up with Science: Speed*. Milwaukee, Wis.: Gareth Stevens, 1995.

Wiese, Jim. *Roller Coaster Science: 50 Wet, Wacky, Wild, Dizzy Experiments about Things Kids Like Best*. New York: John Wiley & Sons, 1994.

Willis, Shirley. *Tell Me How Fast It Goes*. Danbury, Conn.: Franklin Watts, 1999.

Internet Addresses

The Exploratorium. *The Science Explorer*. n.d. <http://www.exploratorium.edu/science_explorer/>.

Trimpe, Tracy. *The Science Spot Kid Zone*. March 1999. <http://sciencespot.net/Pages/kidzone.html>

Scifair.org, and Gudenas, John W. *The Ultimate Science Fair Resource*. © 2000. <http://www.scifair.org>.

Index